Steamer Cookbook

Delicious Steamer Recipes that are Both Healthy and Delicious

BY

Stephanie Sharp

WWWWWWWWWWWWWWWWWWWWWWWWWWWWWWWWWWWWWWWWWWWWWW

License Notes

wwwwwwwwwwwwwwwwwwwwwwwwwwwwwwwwwwwww

My deepest thanks for buying my book! Now that you have made this investment in time and money, you are now eligible for free e-books on a weekly basis! Once you subscribe by filling in the box below with your email address, you will start to receive free and discounted book offers for unique and informative books. There is nothing more to do! A reminder email will be sent to you a few days before the promotion expires so you will never have to worry about missing out on this amazing deal. Enter your email address below to get started. Thanks again for your purchase!

Just visit the link or scan QR-code to get started!

https://stephanie-sharp.subscribemenow.com

wwwwwwwwwwwwwwwwwwwwwwwwwwwwwwwwwwwwwwww

Table of Contents

Introduction

Congrats on buying your brand new Steamer. Steaming works by boiling water continuously which in turn vaporizes into steam. It is this steam and heat that cooks the food keeping it moist and tender. The food in a steamer makes no contact with the boiling water. The steam circulates around the steaming tiers evenly cooking your food to perfection.

While there are numerous new electrical steamers on the market today, the method of cooking by steam is an ancient one. The Chinese have been using steam to cook for more than 3000 years and even today it is still widely used on a daily basis. In the west, steaming is more often used to cook vegetables and fish however there are many rice, meat and poultry dishes that are perfect for the steamer. Our recipes include a fantastic mix of vegetable, seafood and meat dishes.

wwwwwwwwwwwwwwwwwwwwwwwwwwwwwwwwwwww

Steamers

There are different options to choose when steaming your food. Below is a brief description of each.

Electric Steamers

These are the most popular steamers and are very reasonably priced. The benefit of using an electric steamer is that it heats up the water and begins to steam almost immediately so is a quicker method of cooking. It also means your hob/stove top is free (and clean!). All electric steamers come with a timer so your food will not overcook meaning you can leave the device to do its job while you get on with other things. There are different sizes of appliances ranging from single tier to two or three tiers to suit larger families. Most have see-through plastic tiers so you can watch your food cooking and are generally dishwasher friendly.

Stove Top Steamers

These work on the same principle as electric steamers. A large pan forms the base in which water is brought to the boil. There are a further two or three tiers that sit on top of this pan where food is placed to steam. Generally, you cannot see food in these tiers as they are stainless steel although the top tier will usually have a see-through glass lid.

wwwwwwwwwwwwwwwwwwwwwwwwwwwwwwwwwwww

Bamboo Steamers

Popular in Asian cooking, bamboo steamers are predominantly used over boiling water in a wok but can also be used with a pan. These can be stacked to provide two or three tiers. The advantage of bamboo steamers is that they are cheap to buy and the bamboo absorbs moisture that might normally condense on the underside of the steamer lid.

The disadvantage to this type of steaming is that they are difficult to clean, cannot be placed in the dishwasher and the bamboo may absorb and retain the flavor of the food you are cooking.

As with any kitchen appliance, convenience, suitability, reliability, performance and price are all factors in deciding which one works best for you.

wwwwwwwwwwwwwwwwwwwwwwwwwwwwwwwwwww

Delicious Steamer Recipes

wwwwwwwwwwwwwwwwwwwwwwwwwwwwwwwwwwwwww

Honeyed Carrots Hazelnuts

This delicious steamer dish is perfect for both vegetarians and meat lovers alike.

Serving Size: 2

Cooking Time: 20 minutes

Ingredients:

- 200g/7oz fresh baby carrots
- 1 bunch spring onions/scallions
- 1 tbsp clear honey
- 1 tbsp hazelnuts, chopped
- Salt pepper to taste

Directions:

1. Scrub the carrots and halve lengthways, along with the spring onions.

2. Place into the bottom tier of the steamer, cover with the lid and steam for 10 minutes.

3. Add the honey to a ramekin dish, cover tightly with foil and place on a tier above the steaming carrots to gently soften.

4. Cover the steamer back over with the lid and continue to steam the carrots for a further

5. 10 minutes, or until the carrots and spring onions are cooked through and tender. Place in a bowl, pour over the softened honey and combine well.

6. Sprinkle with the chopped hazelnuts and serve.

7. Try using chopped almonds in place of hazelnuts. Enjoy!

wwwwwwwwwwwwwwwwwwwwwwwwwwwwwwwwwwwwwww

Lemon Oil Asparagus

Your steamer gives you tender, and delicious asparagus.

Serving Size: 2

Cooking Time: 18 minutes

Ingredients:

- 200g/7oz asparagus tips
- 1 tbsp lemon juice
- 1 tsp olive oil
- Salt pepper to taste

Directions:

1. Place the asparagus tips on the bottom tier of the steamer, cover with the lid and steam for 10-12 minutes or until tender.

2. Mix the olive oil and juice together. Place the asparagus in a bowl, pour over the lemon oil, combine well, season and serve.

3. A little grated Parmesan cheese makes a good addition to this simple side dish.

Basil Zucchini

These tasty zucchini slices are infused with basil and super delish.

Serving Size: 2

Cooking Time: 15 minutes

Ingredients:

- 3 medium courgettes, sliced
- 1 tbsp lemon juice
- 1 tbsp olive oil
- 2 tbsp freshly chopped basil
- Salt pepper to taste

Directions:

1. Place the sliced courgettes on the bottom tier of the steamer, cover with the lid and steam for 5-7 minutes or until tender.

2. Mix the lemon juice olive oil together.

3. Place the steamed courgettes slices in a bowl and pour over the lemon oil. Combine well, sprinkle with fresh basil, season and serve.

4. Try cutting the courgettes lengthways into long thick slices rather than into discs.

Mangetout With Pine Nuts Mint

This delicious dinner plate is filled with nutrition an easy to whip up in your steamer.

Serving Size: 2

Cooking Time: 15 minutes

Ingredients:

- 200g/7oz mangetout
- 1 tbsp olive oil
- 1 tbsp fresh mint, finely chopped
- 1 tbsp pine nuts
- Salt pepper to taste

Directions:

1. Place the mangetout on the bottom tier of the steamer, cover with the lid and steam for 5-7 minutes or until tender.

2. Meanwhile, very gently toast the pine nuts in a dry frying pan for a couple of minutes until browned (be careful not to burn them).

3. Mix the olive oil and mint together.

4. Place the mangetout in a bowl and pour over the minted oil. Combine well, sprinkle with the toasted pine nuts, season and serve.

5. Sugar snap peas will work equally well for recipe. Enjoy!

wwwwwwwwwwwwwwwwwwwwwwwwwwwwwwwwwwwwwwwww

Salad Potatoes Dijon Vinaigrette

Here is a tasty potato salad with a tasty Vinaigrette.

Serving Size: 2

Cooking Time: 30 minutes

Ingredients:

- 500g/1lb 2oz small salad potatoes
- 1 tbsp lemon juice
- ½ garlic clove, crushed
- 1 tbsp Dijon mustard
- 1 tbsp olive oil
- 1 bunch spring onions/scallions, chopped
- Salt pepper to taste

Directions:

1. Slice the potatoes in half and place in the steamer on the bottom tier.

2. Cover with the lid and steam for 15-20 minutes or until the potatoes are tender.

3. Meanwhile combine the lemon juice, garlic, mustard and oil together in a bowl with a good pinch of salt to make a basic vinaigrette dressing.

4. When the potatoes are tender add to the dressing and combine well.

5. Season and serve with the spring onions scattered over the top.

6. Charlotte potatoes are a good choice for this recipe.

wwwwwwwwwwwwwwwwwwwwwwwwwwwwwwwwwwwwwwww

Purple Sprouting Broccoli Anchovies

Enjoy this tasty dish filled with nutrients for either lunch or a late evening snack.

Serving Size: 2

Cooking Time: 20 minutes

Ingredients:

- 200g/7oz purple sprouting broccoli
- 1 tbsp olive oil
- 2 anchovy fillets or 1 tsp anchovy paste
- 1 garlic clove, crushed
- Salt pepper to taste

Directions:

1. Place the broccoli into the bottom tier of the steamer. Add the oil, anchovy fillets and garlic to a ramekin dish.

2. Cover tightly with foil and place on a tier above the broccoli.

3. Cover the steamer with the lid and steam for 8-10 minutes or until the broccoli is tender.

4. Give the anchovies and oil a good stir to break up the fillets. Place the broccoli in a bowl, pour over the warmed anchovy oil.

5. Combine well, season and serve.

6. Use tender stem broccoli if you can't find purple sprouting broccoli. Enjoy!

wwwwwwwwwwwwwwwwwwwwwwwwwwwwwwwwwwwwwwww

Steamed Savoy with Bacon

This steamed savoy is buttery, flavorful and delicious.

Serving Size: 2

Cooking Time: 25 minutes

Ingredients:

- ½ savoy cabbage, shredded
- 1 tsp low fat 'butter' spread
- 4 slices lean, back bacon
- Salt pepper to taste

Directions:

1. Preheat the grill to a medium heat.

2. Place the shredded cabbage into the bottom tier of the steamer. Cover with the lid and steam for 10-15 minutes or until the cabbage is tender.

3. Meanwhile grill the bacon slices for a few minutes until cooked through. Finely slice and

4. place in a bowl.

5. Add cabbage, ‘butter’ and plenty of black pepper to the bacon. Combine well. Check the seasoning and serve.

6. You could also make this simple side dish using chopped Brussels sprouts. Enjoy!

wwwwwwwwwwwwwwwwwwwwwwwwwwwwwwwwwww

Cumin Turmeric Cauliflower

This tasty Indian inspired cauliflower is perfect for dinner or lunch.

Serving Size: 2

Cooking Time: 22 minutes

Ingredients:

- 300g/11oz cauliflower florets
- 1 tsp each ground cumin turmeric
- 2 tbsp fat free Greek yogurt
- 2 tsp lemon juice
- Salt pepper to taste

Directions:

1. Combine the cauliflower florets, cumin, turmeric a pinch of salt together, making sure the dry spices evenly coat the florets.

2. Place the spiced florets into the bottom tier of the steamer. Cover with the lid and steam for 10-12 minutes or until tender. Remove from the steamer and leave to cool for a minute.

3. Mix together the yogurt and lemon juice in a bowl. Add the cauliflower florets. Combine well, season and serve.

4. Leaving the cauliflower to cool for a minute discourages the excess steam from spoiling/splitting the yogurt dressing. Enjoy!

wwwwwwwwwwwwwwwwwwwwwwwwwwwwwwwwwwwww

Crushed Butternut Squash

If you are seeking a change from average mashed potatoes, give this delicious crushed butternut squash.

Serving Size: 2

Cooking Time: 40 minutes

Ingredients:

- ½ butternut squash, peeled deseeded
- Pinch of salt
- ½ tsp each chopped fresh rosemary thyme
- 1 tsp olive oil
- 1 tbsp low fat cream
- Salt pepper to taste

Directions:

1. Cube the butternut squash and combine with the salt, rosemary, thyme and olive oil.

2. Place in the bottom tier of the steamer. Cover with the lid and steam for 20-30 minutes or until the squash is tender.

3. Remove the squash from the steamer, lightly crush with the back of a fork, add the single cream and combine well. Season and serve.

4. Feel free to use dried herbs if that's all you have to hand. Enjoy!

wwwwwwwwwwwwwwwwwwwwwwwwwwwwwwwwwwwww

Spiced Saffron Lentils

This Saffron Lentil dish is super smooth and delicious.

Serving Size: 2

Cooking Time: 1 hour 15 minutes

Ingredients:

- 125g/4oz lentils
- 370ml/1½ cups hot vegetable stock
- 1 garlic clove, crushed
- ½ tsp each ground coriander/cilantro, cumin turmeric
- Large pinch of saffron threads
- 1 tbsp lemon juice
- ½ tsp each brown sugar salt
- Salt pepper to taste

Directions:

1. Combine all the ingredients in a steam-proof glass bowl.

2. Place the bowl in the bottom tier of the steamer. Cover the steamer with the lid and steam for 50-60 minutes or until the lentils are tender and cooked through. (Stir once or twice during cooking and add additional stock if required).

3. Season and serve.

4. This is tasty as is, or you can serve with your choice of chopped fresh herbs. Enjoy!

wwwwwwwwwwwwwwwwwwwwwwwwwwwwwwwwwwwwwww

Curried Dhal

This delicious curry stew is so tasty that it will quickly become your favorite dinner.

Serving Size: 2

Cooking Time: 1 hour 15 minutes

Ingredients:

- 125g/4oz lentils
- 370ml/1½ cups hot vegetable stock
- 2 garlic cloves, crushed
- 200g/7oz chopped fresh tomatoes
- 200g/7oz carrots, cut into batons
- 1 tbsp medium curry powder
- ½ tsp each brown sugar salt
- 1 tbsp mango chutney
- 1 onion, chopped
- Salt pepper to taste

Directions:

1. Combine all the ingredients, except the mango chutney chopped onion, in a steam-proof glass bowl.

2. Place the bowl in the bottom tier of the steamer. Cover the steamer with the lid and steam for 50-60 minutes or until the lentils are tender and cooked through. (Stir once or twice during cooking and add additional stock if required).

3. Combine together the mango chutney and chopped onion.

4. Season and serve the cooked dhal with a dollop of the mango chutney and chopped onion on the side.

5. Use hot curry powder if you prefer.

wwwwwwwwwwwwwwwwwwwwwwwwwwwwwwwwwwwww

Lime Coconut Lentils

This citrusy lentil dish is fluffy and delicious.

Serving Size: 2

Cooking Time: 1 hour 20 minutes

Ingredients:

- 125g lentils
- 1 tbsp coconut cream
- 1½ cups hot vegetable stock
- 1 tbsp freshly chopped cilantro
- 1 onion, chopped
- Zest of ½ lime
- garlic, 2 cloves, crushed
- 1 tbsp medium curry powder
- ½ tsp each brown sugar salt
- 1 tbsp lime juice
- Salt pepper to taste

Directions:

1. Combine all the ingredients, except the coconut cream and chopped coriander, in a steam-proof glass bowl.

2. Place the bowl in the bottom tier of the steamer. Cover the steamer with the lid and steam for 50-60 minutes or until the lentils are tender and cooked through. (Stir once or twice during cooking and add additional stock if required).

3. When the lentils are tender, stir through the coconut cream, sprinkle with chopped coriander and serve.

4. Add more lime juice to suit your own taste. Enjoy!

wwwwwwwwwwwwwwwwwwwwwwwwwwwwwwwwwwwwwwww

Sweet Potato Split Peas

This creamy Sweet Potato dish is part chunky, part smooth and all delicious.

Serving Size: 2

Cooking Time: 1 hour 35 minutes

Ingredients:

- 125g/4oz yellow split peas
- 370ml/1½ cups hot vegetable stock
- 1 onion, chopped
- 250g/9oz sweet potato, peeled diced
- 1 garlic clove, crushed
- 1 tsp each garam masala turmeric
- ½ tsp cayenne pepper
- 75g/3oz spinach
- Salt pepper to taste

Directions:

1. Combine all the ingredients, except the spinach, in a steam-proof glass bowl.

2. Place the bowl in the bottom tier of the steamer. Cover the steamer with the lid and steam for 70-80 minutes or until the split peas are tender and cooked through. (Stir once or twice during cooking and add additional stock if required).

3. When the peas are ready, stir through the spinach for a few seconds and serve.

4. Combine the spinach with the peas for a little longer if you prefer it wilted. Enjoy!

wwwwwwwwwwwwwwwwwwwwwwwwwwwwwwwwwwww

Subzi Dalcha

Here we have a tasty soup that would be perfect for lunch or dinner.

Serving Size: 2

Cooking Time: 1 hour 35 minutes

Ingredients:

- 4oz yellow split peas
- 1½ cups hot vegetable stock
- 11oz mixed vegetables
- 2 garlic cloves, crushed
- 2 tsp turmeric
- 1 tsp cumin
- ½ tsp ground ginger chili powder
- 3 curry leaves
- 2 tbsp fat free Greek Yogurt
- ½ - 1 red chili, deseeded finely chopped
- Salt pepper to taste

Directions:

1. Combine all the ingredients, except the yogurt and chopped chili, in a steam-proof glass bowl.

2. Place the bowl in the bottom tier of the steamer. Cover the steamer with the lid and steam for 70-80 minutes or until the split peas are tender and cooked through. (Stir once or twice during cooking and add additional stock if required). Top up the water level on your steamer as required.

3. When the peas are ready, remove the curry leaves and serve with a dollop of yogurt in the center of the dish sprinkled with fresh chopped chilies.

4. Use any combination of mixed vegetables you prefer – even a frozen prepared mix will work well. Enjoy!

wwwwwwwwwwwwwwwwwwwwwwwwwwwwwwwwwwwww

Bulgar Wheat Warm Tabbouleh

For a tasty grain dish that will leave you longing for more, give this Bulgar Wheat Tabbouleh.

Serving Size: 2

Cooking Time: 1 hour 30 minutes

Ingredients:

- 125g/4oz bulgar wheat
- 250ml/1 cup hot vegetable stock
- ½ red onion, chopped
- Pinch of ground cinnamon
- 1 tbsp lemon juice
- 2 fresh tomatoes chopped
- Large bunch of freshly chopped herbs
- Lemon wedges to serve
- Salt pepper to taste

Directions:

1. Combine all the ingredients, except the chopped herbs and lemon wedges, in a steam-proof glass bowl.

2. Place the bowl in the bottom tier of the steamer. Cover the steamer with the lid and steam for 30-40 minutes or until the bulgar wheat is tender and cooked through. (Stir once during cooking and add additional stock if required).

3. When the wheat is ready, fluff it up with a fork and leave to cool for a few minutes. Quickly fold through the chopped herbs and serve with lemon wedges.

4. Equal quantities of mint, basil and flat leaf parsley make a good combination of fresh herbs for this dish. Enjoy!

wwwwwwwwwwwwwwwwwwwwwwwwwwwwwwwwwwwwwww

Savory Spiced Steamed Rice

This delicious rice dish can easily serve as a full dish on its own or as a delish side.

Serving Size: 2

Cooking Time: 50 minutes

Ingredients:

- 150g/5oz basmati rice
- 370ml/1½ cups hot vegetable stock
- 1 onion, chopped
- 1 garlic clove, crushed
- 75g/3oz peas
- 75g/3oz sliced mushrooms
- 1 red pepper, deseeded chopped
- 1 tbsp medium curry powder
- 2 fresh tomatoes, chopped
- Salt pepper to taste

Directions:

1. Combine all the ingredients in a steam-proof glass bowl.

2. Place the bowl in the bottom tier of the steamer.

3. Cover the steamer with the lid and cook for 30-35 minutes or until the rice is tender. (Stir only once during cooking and add additional stock if required).

4. When the rice is ready, check the seasoning and serve.

5. Try serving with some chopped spring onions sprinkled over the top. Enjoy!

wwwwwwwwwwwwwwwwwwwwwwwwwwwwwwwwwwwwww

Pomegranate Mint Quinoa

This sweet and spiced quinoa is fluffy and delicious.

Serving Size: 2

Cooking Time: 45 minutes

Ingredients:

- 100g/3½oz quinoa
- 370ml/1½ cups hot vegetable stock
- 1 tsp lemon juice
- 1 bunch mint, finely chopped
- Seeds from 2 whole pomegranates
- Salt pepper to taste

Directions:

1. Combine the quinoa and stock in a steam-proof glass bowl.

2. Place the bowl in the bottom tier of the steamer. Cover the steamer with the lid and cook for 30-35 minutes or until the quinoa is tender and the stock has been absorbed. (Stir only once during cooking and add additional stock if required).

3. When the quinoa is ready fluff it up with a fork and toss through the lemon juice, mint and pomegranate seeds. Season and serve.

4. Garnish with your pomegranate seeds and serve. Enjoy!

wwwwwwwwwwwwwwwwwwwwwwwwwwwwwwwwwww

Cantonese Fish Coriander Rice

This tasty Cantonese Fish dish is mildly spicy and makes the perfect dinner.

Serving Size: 2

Cooking Time: 55 minutes

Ingredients:

- 100g/3½oz long grain rice
- 250ml/1 cup vegetable stock
- 2 firm white fish fillets, each weighing 150g/5oz
- ½ tsp coarse sea salt
- 1 tsp freshly grated ginger
- 1 tsp sesame oil
- 2 tbsp soy sauce
- Large bunch spring onions/scallions sliced lengthways
- 4 tbsp freshly chopped coriander/cilantro
- Salt pepper to taste

Directions:

1. Combine the rice stock in a steam-proof glass bowl and place in the second tier of the steamer.

2. Cover the steamer with the lid and steam for 20 minutes.

3. Meanwhile rub the sea salt into the fish fillets. Mix together the oil ginger and brush evenly over the top of the fish.

4. Place the fish side by side on a large piece of tin foil. Fold the foil into a loose parcel leaving enough room for the steam to circulate freely around the top and sides of the fillets.

5. Put the foil parcel in the bottom tier of the steamer. Cover with the lid and steam for 10-15 minutes or until the fish is cooked through and the rice is tender. (Stir the rice only once during cooking and add additional stock if required.)

6. When the rice is cooked, fluff it up with a fork and fold through the chopped coriander.

7. Arrange the fillets on a plate with the rice on the side. Spoon the soy sauce over the fish and scatter with spring onions. Serve immediately.

8. Cod or sole fillets work well for this recipe. Enjoy!

wwwwwwwwwwwwwwwwwwwwwwwwwwwwwwwwwwwww

Steamed Salmon Watercress Rice

This delicious dish makes a perfect family dinner for two.

Serving Size: 2

Cooking Time: 400

Ingredients:

- 3½oz long grain rice
- 1 cup boiling water
- Large pinch of salt
- 2 boneless salmon fillets, each weighing 5oz
- 2 tsp lemon juice
- 2 tbsp white wine
- Large handful fresh watercress, chopped
- Salt pepper to taste

Directions:

1. Combine the rice, water salt in a steam-proof glass bowl and place in the second tier of the steamer. Cover the steamer with the lid and steam for 20 minutes.

2. Place the fish fillets side by side on a large piece of tin foil, season well and pour over the lemon juice white wine.

3. Fold the foil into a loose parcel leaving enough room for the steam to circulate freely around the top and sides of the fillets.

4. Place the foil parcel in the bottom tier of the steamer. Cover with the lid and steam for 10-15 minutes or until the fish is cooked through and the rice is tender. (Stir the rice only once during cooking and add additional water if required.)

5. When the rice is cooked fluff it up with a fork and quickly combine with the chopped watercress.

6. Arrange the fillets on a plate with the rice on the side. Spoon any juices from the foil over the fish and serve.

7. Chopped chives are also good added to the cooked rice. Enjoy!

wwwwwwwwwwwwwwwwwwwwwwwwwwwwwwwwwwww

Cod with Rosemary Tomatoes

This flaky Cod will blow your mind with its delicious flavor and ease to prepare.

Serving Size: 2

Cooking Time: 28 minutes

Ingredients:

- 2 firm white fish fillets, each weighing 175g/6oz
- 1 garlic clove, crushed
- 4 vine ripened tomatoes, sliced
- 1 tsp freshly chopped rosemary
- ½ tsp brown sugar
- 150g/5oz rocket
- 1 tbsp low fat mayonnaise
- Salt pepper to taste

Directions:

1. Place the garlic, sliced tomatoes, rosemary and sugar in a small bowl and gently combine.

2. Place the fish fillets side by side on a large piece of tin foil. Season the fish and lay the dressed tomatoes over the top of the fillets.

3. Fold the foil into a loose parcel leaving enough room for the steam to circulate freely around the top and sides of the fillets.

4. Place in the bottom tier of the steamer. Cover with the lid and steam for 15-18 minutes or until the fish is cooked through and the tomatoes are tender.

5. Arrange the fish and tomatoes on a plate, with the rocket on the side along with a dollop of low fat mayo.

6. Dried rosemary is also fine to use with this recipe. Enjoy!

wwwwwwwwwwwwwwwwwwwwwwwwwwwwwwwwww

Steamed Garlic Prawns

These tasty prawns are laced with an essence of garlic and is delicious.

Serving Size: 2

Cooking Time: 45 minutes

Ingredients:

- 100g/3½oz long grain rice
- 250ml/1 cup boiling water
- Large pinch of salt
- 400g/14oz raw, shelled king prawns/jumbo shrimp
- 3 garlic cloves, crushed
- 1 tbsp olive oil
- Lemon Wedges to serve
- 2 tbsp chopped flat leaf parsley
- Salt pepper to taste

Directions:

1. Combine the rice, water salt in a steam-proof glass bowl and place in the second tier of the steamer. Cover the steamer with the lid and steam for 25 minutes.

2. Combine the prawns, garlic oil together and place on a large piece of tin foil.

3. Season well and fold the foil into a loose parcel leaving enough room for the steam to circulate freely around the top and sides of the prawns.

4. Place the foil parcel in the bottom tier of the steamer. Cover with the lid and steam for 5-10 minutes or until the prawns are cooked through and the rice is tender. (Stir the rice only once during cooking and add additional water if required.)

5. When the rice is cooked, fluff it up with a fork and place in shallow bowls.

6. Pile the cooked prawns on top, sprinkle over the chopped parsley and serve with lemon wedges.

7. Fresh peas tossed though the rice is great with this simple supper. Enjoy!

wwwwwwwwwwwwwwwwwwwwwwwwwwwwwwwwwwwwww

Shrimp Pineapple Rice

This Asian inspired Shrimp and Pineapple rice is so delicious you will never long for take out again.

Serving Size: 2

Cooking Time: 46 minutes

Ingredients:

- 3½oz long grain rice
- 1 cup hot vegetable stock
- 11oz raw, shelled king prawns/jumbo shrimp
- 5oz peas
- 4oz pineapple chunks, chopped
- 1 tbsp soy sauce
- Salt pepper to taste

Directions:

1. Combine the rice stock in a steam-proof glass bowl and place in the second tier of the steamer. Cover the steamer with the lid and steam for 25 minutes.

2. Place the prawns, peas pineapple in the bottom tier of the steamer.

3. Cover with the lid and steam for 5-10 minutes or until the prawns are cooked through and the rice is tender. (Stir the rice only once during cooking and add additional stock if required.)

4. Toss everything, including the soy sauce, together. Check the seasoning and serve.

5. If you are using frozen peas, they may need a little longer in the steamer, make sure they are tender before serving. Enjoy!

wwwwwwwwwwwwwwwwwwwwwwwwwwwwwwwwwwwwwwwwww

Steamed Prawns Couscous

This complete dish can be made in your steamer and can be enjoyed on just about any night of the week.

Serving Size: 2

Cooking Time: 30 minutes

Ingredients:

- 2 red chilies, deseeded
- 2 garlic cloves
- 1 tbsp olive oil
- 1 tbsp lemon juice
- 1 tbsp white wine vinegar
- ½ tsp salt
- 300g/11oz raw, shelled king prawns/jumbo shrimp
- 100g/3½oz couscous
- 180ml/¾ cup hot vegetable stock
- 50g/2oz rocket
- Salt pepper to taste

Directions:

1. Add the chilies, garlic, olive oil, lemon juice, vinegar salt to a food processor and whizz into a paste.

2. Remove the blade, add the prawns and combine well.

3. Put the couscous stock in a steam-proof glass bowl and stir once. Place the chili-covered prawns on top of the couscous and put the bowl in the bottom tier of the steamer.

4. Cover the steamer with the lid and steam for 5-10 minutes or until the prawns are cooked through.

5. Use a fork to fluff up the couscous and toss everything well. Serve with the rocket piled on top.

6. Adjust the chili to suit your own taste in this spicy dish. Enjoy!

wwwwwwwwwwwwwwwwwwwwwwwwwwwwwwwwwwww

Dressed Yogurt Chicken Breasts

This Dressed Yogurt Chicken Breasts are juicy and delicious.

Serving Size: 2

Cooking Time: 30 minutes

Ingredients:

- 2 chicken breasts, each weighing 5oz
- 1 tsp dried thyme
- 1 lemon, thinly sliced
- 2 garlic cloves, peeled
- 9oz asparagus tips
- 2 tbsp fat free Greek yogurt
- 1 tsp Dijon mustard
- 1 tsp clear honey
- Salt pepper to taste

Directions:

1. Season the chicken breasts, sprinkle with thyme and place on the bottom tier of the steamer.

2. Place the garlic cloves in there too and then cover the chicken breasts with the lemon slices.

3. Cover with the lid and leave to steam for 10 minutes. After this timc placc the asparagus tips in the second tier and steam for 10 minutes longer or until the chicken is cooked through and the asparagus is tender.

4. Remove the steamed garlic and crush. Gently combine this with the yogurt, mustard honey to make a dressing.

5. Arrange the chicken and asparagus on the plate and serve with the yogurt dressing poured over the chicken breast.

6. Include some of the lemon slices from the steamer on the plate if you wish. Enjoy!

wwwwwwwwwwwwwwwwwwwwwwwwwwwwwwwwwww

Lemongrass Ginger Chicken

Enjoy this tasty Ginger and Lemongrass recipe as a dinner dish or even as your next lunch.

Serving Size: 2

Cooking Time: 35 minutes

Ingredients:

- 1 tsp fish sauce
- 1 garlic clove, crushed
- 1 tsp soy sauce
- 1 red chili, deseeded finely chopped
- 1 tsp freshly grated ginger
- 1 tbsp clear honey
- 1 lemongrass stalk, finely chopped
- 2 chicken breasts, each weighing 150g/5oz
- 5oz peas
- 3½oz long grain rice
- 1 cup boiling water
- Large pinch of salt
- Salt pepper to taste

Directions:

1. Combine together the fish sauce, garlic, soy, chili, ginger, honey and chopped lemongrass to make a marinade.

2. Use your hands to rub the marinade into the chicken breast and put to one side to allow the flavor to develop.

3. Meanwhile combine the rice, water salt in a steam-proof glass bowl and place in the second tier of the steamer. Cover the steamer with the lid and steam for 10 minutes.

4. Add the marinated chicken breasts to the bottom tier of the steamer and add the peas to the steam-proof bowl with the rice.

5. Cover the steamer and leave to cook for a further 20 minutes or until the chicken is cooked through and the rice tender.

6. Cut the chicken into thick slices and use a fork to fluff up the pea rice. Serve in shallow bowls with the chicken slices on top of the rice.

7. Try spinach or sugar snaps peas in the rice if you like. Enjoy!

wwwwwwwwwwwwwwwwwwwwwwwwwwwwwwwwwww

Honey Chicken with Savory Lentils

This Honey laced chicken is succulent and juicy with savory lentils that you will be bound to enjoy.

Serving Size: 2

Cooking Time: 30 minutes

Ingredients:

- 3 ½oz lentils
- 1 cup hot vegetable stock
- 2 chicken breasts, each weighing 5oz
- 1 tsp clear honey
- 1 tsp soy sauce
- 2 tbsp freshly chopped basil
- Salt pepper to taste

Directions:

1. Combine the lentils and stock in a steam-proof glass bowl and place on the second tier of the steamer.

2. Cover the steamer with the lid and cook for 40 minutes.

3. Brush the chicken breasts with the honey and soy sauce, place in the bottom tier of the steamer, cover and cook for a further 20 minutes or until the chicken is cooked through and the lentils are tender (stir the lentils once or twice during cooking and add additional stock if required).

4. Cut the chicken breasts into thick slices and serve with the lentils on the side sprinkled with fresh basil.

5. Red lentils are best for this recipe. Enjoy!

wwwwwwwwwwwwwwwwwwwwwwwwwwwwwwwwwwwwwwwww

Steamed Chicken Lemon Spinach

This delicious entrée will be a great choice for any day of the week.

Serving Size: 2

Cooking Time: 33 minutes

Ingredients:

- 2 chicken breasts, each weighing 5oz
- 2 garlic cloves, crushed
- 1 tsp olive oil
- 2 courgettes, thinly sliced lengthways
- ½ onion, finely chopped
- 5oz spinach
- 2 tsp lemon juice
- Salt pepper to taste

Directions:

1. Place the chicken breasts side by side on a large piece of tin foil. Mix together the garlic olive oil and brush over the chicken fillets.

2. Lay the courgettes slices and chopped onions on top of the chicken and fold the foil into a loose parcel leaving enough room for the steam to circulate freely around the top and sides of the chicken breasts and courgettes.

3. Place in the bottom tier of the steamer. Cover with the lid and steam for 20 minutes or until the chicken is cooked through.

4. Add the spinach to the second tier of the steamer, cover and steam for a further 2-3 minutes or until the spinach has wilted.

5. Transfer the spinach to a bowl, toss with the lemon juice and a good pinch of salt.

6. Remove the chicken and courgette parcel from the steamer and serve on plates with the spinach on the side.

7. Try garnishing the spinach with sesame seeds and a little extra olive oil.

wwwwwwwwwwwwwwwwwwwwwwwwwwwwwwwwwwwwwww

Lean Quarter Pounder

This Lean Quarter pounder is juicy and delicious.

Serving Size: 2

Cooking Time: 25 minutes

Ingredients:

- 9oz lean beef minced beef
- 1 garlic clove (crushed)
- 1 egg (beaten)
- 1 tsp Worcestershire sauce
- 1 tsp Dijon Mustard
- 2 slices low fat cheddar cheese
- 1 vine ripened tomato (sliced)
- 1 baby gem lettuce (shredded)
- 2 regular wholemeal burger rolls
- Salt pepper to taste

Directions:

1. Place the beef, garlic, egg, Worcestershire sauce and mustard into a bowl. Mix well and form into two burger patties.

2. Place the burgers in the bottom tier of the steamer, cover with the lid and steam for 10-15 minutes or until the burgers are cooked through.

3. Place the cheese on top of the burgers and steam for a couple of minutes (if you want the cheese melted).

4. To serve; assemble the burgers in the rolls with the shredded lettuce sliced tomatoes.

5. Try using a plastic burger maker. They are cheap to buy and vastly improve the texture of the burger.

wwwwwwwwwwwwwwwwwwwwwwwwwwwwwwwwwwwwwww

Steamed Citrus Pork

A nutritious dinner for two. Tender pork loins flavored with citrus juice, honey and coriander.

Serving Size: 2

Cooking Time: 35 minutes

Ingredients:

- 2 pork loin steaks (each weighing 5oz)
- 2 tbsp orange juice
- 1 tbsp coriander (freshly chopped)
- 7oz carrots (cut into batons)
- 1 tsp clear honey
- 2 tsp lemon juice
- Salt pepper to taste

Directions:

1. Place the pork loins side by side on a large piece of foil. Season well and pour over the orange juice and chopped coriander.

2. Fold the foil into a loose parcel leaving enough room for the steam to circulate freely around the top and sides of the pork steaks.

3. Place the carrot batons in a bowl and combine with the honey. Place the foil parcels in the bottom tier of the steamer and the carrots in the second tier.

4. Cover with the lid and steam for 18-25 minutes or until the pork is cooked through and the carrots are tender.

5. This is also good served with some roasted gnocchi.

wwwwwwwwwwwwwwwwwwwwwwwwwwwwwwwwwwwwwwww

Pineapple Banana Rafts

This quick, easy and fancy fruit salad goes together quite nicely. A very attractive and healthy appetizer.

Serving Size: 2

Cooking Time: 20 minutes

Ingredients:

- 1 banana (sliced)
- 2 tinned pineapple rings
- 4 glace cherries (chopped)
- 1 tsp brown sugar
- 2 tbsp fat free Greek yogurt

Directions:

1. Cut out two pieces of foil and lay a pineapple slice on each piece. Place the sliced banana on top of the rings along with the cherries and the brown sugar.

2. Fold the foil into two loose parcels making sure there is enough space around the side and top of the pineapple ring for the steam to circulate.

3. Place the parcels in the bottom tier of the steamer and steam for 15 minutes. Serve with a dollop of fat free Greek yogurt.

4. Double the pineapple rings in the rafts if you want a larger dessert.

wwwwwwwwwwwwwwwwwwwwwwwwwwwwwwwwwwwww

Conclusion

Congrats on completing all 30 delicious Steamer Recipes! We hope you enjoyed all 30 recipes and that they were easy to whip up and tasty.

So, what happens next?

In order to become better at making steamers you will have to practice. Be sure to keep cooking and enjoying all the delicious recipes featured in this Creative Steamer Cookbook. All of which will be easy to follow and can be created in a hassle-free environment. So, whenever you feel like you have mastered all the recipes in this book, grab another one of our books and let your culinary creativity run wild.

Remember, drop us a review if you loved what you read and until we meet again, keep on cooking delicious food.

wwwwwwwwwwwwwwwwwwwwwwwwwwwwwwwwwwwwwwwww

About the Author

Born in New Germantown, Pennsylvania, Stephanie Sharp received a Masters degree from Penn State in English Literature. Driven by her passion to create culinary masterpieces, she applied and was accepted to The International Culinary School of the Art Institute where she excelled in French cuisine. She has married her cooking skills with an aptitude for business by opening her own small cooking school where she teaches students of all ages.

Stephanie's talents extend to being an author as well and she has written over 400 e-books on the art of cooking and baking that include her most popular recipes.

Sharp has been fortunate enough to raise a family near her hometown in Pennsylvania where she, her husband and children live in a beautiful rustic house on an extensive piece of land. Her other passion is taking care of the furry members of her family which include 3 cats, 2 dogs and a potbelly pig named Wilbur.

Watch for more amazing books by Stephanie Sharp coming out in the next few months.

Author's Afterthoughts

I am truly grateful to you for taking the time to read my book. I cherish all of my readers! Thanks ever so much to each of my cherished readers for investing the time to read this book!

With so many options available to you, your choice to buy my book is an honour, so my heartfelt thanks at reading it from beginning to end!

I value your feedback, so please take a moment to submit an honest and open review on Amazon so I can get valuable insight into my readers' opinions and others can benefit from your experience.

Thank you for taking the time to review!

Stephanie Sharp

For announcements about new releases, please follow my author page on Amazon.com!

(Look for the Follow Bottom under the photo)

You can find that at:

https://www.amazon.com/author/stephanie-sharp

*or Scan **QR-code** below.*

Made in the USA
Monee, IL
11 February 2021